No Bones about It Archaeology for Kids!

Science for Children Edition
Children's Archaeology Books

pfiffikus

EDUCATIONAL BOOKS FOR CHILDREN K-12

Archaeology is defined as the study of humans through the recovery and analysis of archaeological records.

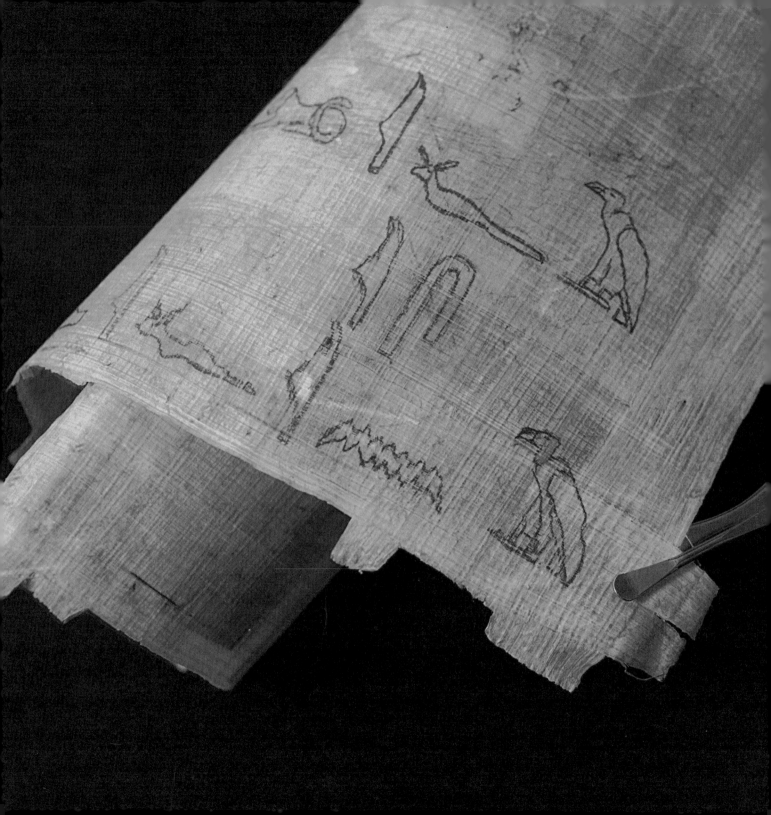

These archaeological records include artifacts, bio-facts and even the cultural landscapes.

Archaeologists
follow a pattern
when they dig.
Let us show you
how they do it!

This tutorial will provide you with an outline of how to dig a test pit to find some archaeological records in your own backyard. There are three stages to remember.

First stage: Preparation

I.   Research on history first. Check your local library or museum to make sure you have a clear perspective of what you can expect to find.

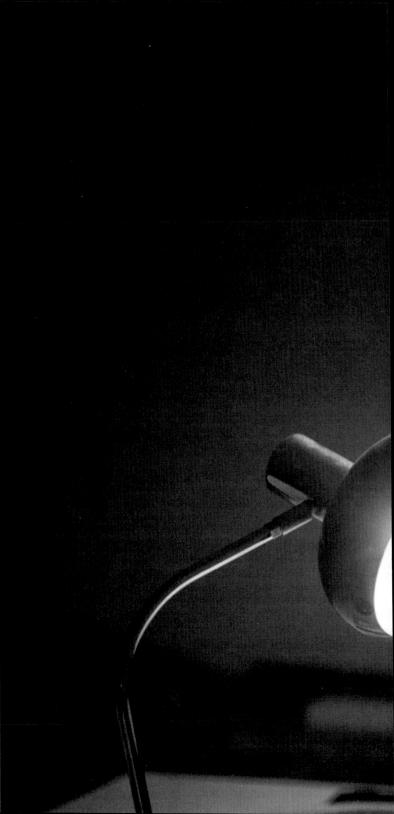

2. Check your backyard for earthworks and signs. These signs may include traces of ploughing and terracing. Some other signs that you can look out for are parch marks in grass fields and natural stones.

3. Observe the local landscape. You may analyze why people have decided to dwell in that particular place.

4. Look for the perfect digging site in your own backyard or in other nearby areas.

Second Stage: Starting the Trench

1. Gather your tools. The main tools that you will need include a shovel, a garden trowel or a cement trowel if available, a brush, a scraper, a camera and a yardstick or ruler.

2. Dig a test pit. recommended measurement should not exceed one meter across. Start to measure with a string. Check the first layer of soil. If there are interesting finds like old coin, take a photograph for your record.

3. Start taking one layer of soil back and so on.

4. Observe
soil changes.
Stratigraphy refers
to the study of
complex layers,
and this is greatly
connected to
paleontology.

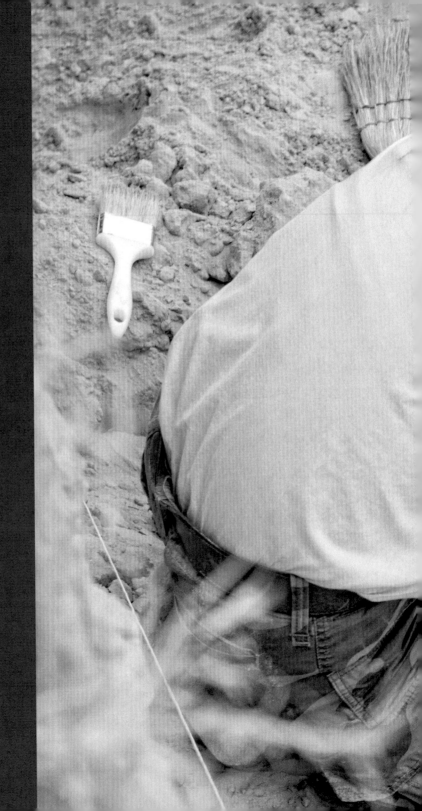

5. Dig where the evidence would take you.

Third Stage: Conclude the Dig

1. Record any data that came from this trench. Take a photograph of every layer or anytime there is an interesting find.

The data you record today can be very significant to local historians in the future.

Take note that
every object that
you find may
help rebuild the
picture of their life
way back then.

Being an archaeologist is no easy task. But with great passion and these tips, you can become a kiddie archaeologist, too!